*My journal pages, sometimes
stained with tears and often
penned in
early-morning hours, hold trea-
sured fragments from my spiritual
journey— the lessons that He
taught me, the joy that stirred in my
soul, the secret things
I told Him, knowing He wouldn't
turn away.
As I look back, I see traces
of the barren stretches when I could
not speak, and feel the thrill of new
beginnings. I marvel at His leading,
find assurance of His love, and am
reminded that I am happiest when I
am by His side.*

REVIEW AND HERALD®
PUBLISHING ASSOCIATION
HAGERSTOWN, MARYLAND 21740
COPYRIGHT © 1993

A Note to God !

4-25 2013 - my First
have never been much to wrote
things down. Many times just
don't know what to say.
    Today I say Thank You !!!
You brought joy to someone I
love + again Thank You !!
It is something that has been
needed for a long time. I
was afraid it would come
to late, I know it is not
the end, but a beginning is
good enough for Now ♡
AGAIN THANK You -
I will remember kindness
today